A Doll's House Study Guide

CRACK THE COMPARATIVE #7

GW00683446

Amy Farrell

SCENE BY SCENE

WICKLOW, IRELAND

Scene by Scene
Wicklow, Ireland.
www.scenebyscene.ie

A Doll's House Study Guide by Amy Farrell.
ISBN 978-1-910949-84-9

Contents

About This Book

This book is a study guide for Leaving Certificate English. It provides notes for the Comparative Study of *A Doll's House*, by Henrik Ibsen.

There are notes and analysis of key moments for Cultural Context/ Social Setting, Literary Genre, General Vision and Viewpoint, Theme/Issue (Relationships) and Hero, Heroine, Villain.

I have selected key moments to analyse for each comparative study mode. However, my choices are not definitive - any moment can be considered and explored for any mode. Feel free to consider other moments to add to your analysis for the comparative study.

A Doll's House by Henrik Ibsen

The play tells the story of Nora and Torvald Helmer, and the secret that destroys their marriage and changes their lives, transforming Nora in the process.

Notes on Cultural Context/Social Setting

This is **a world of wealth and privilege**, where Nora and Torvald can afford servants, a beautiful home, and to travel to Italy for a life-saving holiday.

In this world, **women are dependant on their fathers and husbands** to govern their lives for them. Here, **a woman's rightful place is in the home**, being a mother and wife. Women cannot sign legal documents, for that a man's signature is necessary, showing that women are far from equal.

Mrs Linde feels that she lacks a purpose without someone to care for and look after, highlighting **the role of women as mothers and caregivers.**

Mrs Linde's backstory adds to our understanding of the difficulties of being a woman in this world, and the practical side of marriage in this place. She **married for financial security**, to provide for her family rather than for love, and as a widow with no-one to care for, is seeking purpose in her life.

Reputation and social standing are important in this world, **particularly for men**. Torvald's professional position earns him a certain standing and respect. This is Krogstad's motivation for coercing Nora into influencing Torvald to give him back his job at the bank, it is **respect and social standing that he seeks.**

Because of the **significance of one's reputation**, and the **desire to be respectable**, the threat of blackmail, of having one's secrets exposed, is a significant danger to these characters.

When Torvald rejects Nora after learning of her crime, he says that the **pretence of their marriage will continue**, telling her they will act as if nothing has changed in public. It is important to him that **outwardly nothing should change**. His focus is on **maintaining the illusion of a happy marriage**, on **making sure his reputation remains intact**. This tells us **how important appearances are in this world**, while also highlighting that it is Torvald, not Nora, who will determine what happens next in their lives. **Within a marriage, the man is the decision maker, while his wife is supposed to be supportive of his decisions.**

The world of the play is a false and fake place. Nora and Torvald do not care about Dr Rank's illness and approaching death, showing the **falseness of their friendship** with him and a lack of warmth or genuine feeling. Torvald's suggestion that Nora appears as his wife after he rejects her also adds to this idea of **false appearances** and doing things for show.

However, despite the falseness of appearances, this is also **a world where the truth comes out. Nothing remains hidden, everything is revealed and ultimately resolved**. Rank speaks of the sins of his father manifesting as his illness. In this way his father's wrongdoing and hidden desires are exposed. Similarly, Nora's forgery, and the falseness of her marriage are revealed. **Fronts and facades are important in this world, protecting lives and reputations, but it seems they are only ever temporary.**

The position of women is clearly defined in this society; **women are wives and mothers, offering support and care to their husbands and families**. The legal issue of needing a man's signature on documents makes the dependant nature of women clear. This is why Nora's final act, to leave behind her home, husband and family, is so shocking and rebellious. She **rejects her society's conventions in choosing to seek her own identity. This is a startling move in a world where women are so limited by society and conform to society's expectations for them.**

Cultural Context/Social Setting
Key Moments

Opening Scene

The Helmers are a **well-to-do, middle class** couple, with a comfortable, stylish home. They can afford to spend money celebrating Christmas and employing servants. The parcels Nora carries, and her exchanges with her maid and the porter show that she has money, and a certain **social standing** in this world.

Theirs is **a world of order and courtesy;** Nora instructs the maid and tips the porter, things are done as they should be.

Torvald's opening conversation makes clear the position of women in society. **Nora is his squirrel, songbird and featherbrain, a silly favourite pet to be doted on rather than an equal. He even exclaims that Nora is just like a woman when she talks about borrowing money - here, women are not expected to understand anything of business and** finance, this is strictly for the world of men.

In addition to viewing **women** as incapable of engaging in the world of business, they are also viewed as being **childlike and immature.** Torvald asks if his little squirrel is making sulky faces after telling Nora that they shall not borrow. He makes the serious decisions and treats her like a child. **This gives an idea of how women are viewed in this world, as being dependant on the men in their lives to make important decisions, much as children are.**

Mrs Linde's Arrival

Mrs Linde gives an interesting insight into the **values** of this world. She has not had as comfortable and privileged a life as Nora, in fact, Nora does not recognise her at first as she has been so changed by her difficult life.

Mrs Linde's husband died leaving her nothing, not even sad memories. Kristine's marriage has been unhappy, she never loved her husband, only **marrying him to provide security for her family.** Her mother was old and bedridden and she had two younger brothers to support. When the man who became her husband proposed, she felt duty-bound to accept his offer of marriage. Her choice shows the **importance of financial security** to characters, and also **the responsibility Kristine feels towards her family**. Marrying a wealthy man was a way of providing for her family, so she felt duty-bound to marry, despite the lack of love in her life.

Since her husband's death, Kristine has worked at whatever job she can find. Importantly, **she describes her life as empty and meaningless without someone to care for,** saying she has no-one left to live for. This shows how the **role of women in this text is that of mother and caregiver**. Without someone to look after, Mrs Linde feels empty and adrift. She looks for work to fill this void in her life. This is why she has come to Nora, she hopes that Nora will arrange for Torvald to employ her. In this world, **Torvald's work position makes him an influential person.** Kristine hopes that he will use this power to her advantage.

Krogstad Threatens Nora

When Krogstad comes to speak to Nora on Christmas Eve she is defiant and boastful, claiming that she is not without influence just because she is a woman. However, this idea of influence, and being able to use one's power over others is precisely why Krogstad has come to see her, wanting her to influence Torvald on his behalf so that he can keep his position at the bank.

Once again, **the importance of work and financial stability** is clear, Krogstad wants to remain secure, and not lose his job to Mrs Linde. It is his **reputation and social standing** that he wants to preserve.

He has been guilty of a financial indiscretion in the past, he says he slipped up. Although it never came to court, it hindered him and limited his career. This shows the importance of **reputation** in this world. **Characters want to be seen as respectable and upstanding to get on in life, they live in a world of principles**.

Krogstad is blackmailing Nora so that he can appear principled and respectable. He reminds her of the loan she got from him, and the contract that was signed, emphasising that the authenticity of the signature is what is important. Nora has committed forgery by signing this document. **As a woman, she cannot take out a loan like this without a man's signature to guarantee it. This legal situation shows the position of women in society. They lack the legal autonomy of men, barred from** transactions like this without a man's say-so.

Torvald Refuses to Employ Krogstad

The exchange between Nora and Torvald when she asks him to give Krogstad back his job reveals a lot about this world. Nora begins, by asking Torvald whether he would grant his little squirrel something if she asked very, very nicely. She acts the part of childish pet, wheedling and pleading to Torvald who holds the power.
He speaks to her as if she is a naughty child, saying he cannot believe her obstinacy. He is the one who makes decisions in the household, not his wife.

Nora says she is scared of Krogstad, because of things that were written in the paper about her father. This shows that **reputation is something to be protected in this world.**

Torvald tells Nora that her father was not a respected public official like him. **Respect and social standing are important in this world, where reputation matters so much.**

Another significant aspect of this exchange is how Torvald feels people would perceive him if they knew Nora could influence him. He feels he would be a laughing stock in front of his whole staff, that they would think anyone could work on him. Doing as Nora asks would be seen as weakness in this world, **Torvald would be mocked and laughed at if his staff thought his wife could influence him.**

This conversation, and Torvald's refusal to re-employ Krogstad, shows that **Nora, as wife, is part pet, part child in Torvald's eyes.** If people thought he was influenced by her, he would be a joke. This is his reason for refusing to re-hire Krogstad, what people think of him is important to Torvald who wants to be respected.

Torvald Learns of Nora's Crime

When Torvald reads what Nora has done, he turns on her immediately, calling her a criminal. **He judges her very coldly**, saying she has no religion, ethics or sense of duty. Torvald does not see what Nora has done for him, focusing instead on **the impact her actions will have on his reputation and social standing**. He tells her she has destroyed his future. Torvald's reaction is selfish and self-centred, **he thinks of himself, his reputation and career**.

He intends to keep Nora's crime quiet, saying it must be hushed up whatever it costs. This shows how important his **reputation** is to him, he does not want this business between Nora and Krogstad to become public knowledge. **This also shows the hypocrisy and double standards of this world. Torvald thinks Krogstad is deceitful and untrustworthy, but now wants to dishonestly hush up this matter of his own.**

Torvald treats Nora with coldness and indifference, saying that she will stay in the house, but only for appearances sake. He adds that he will not permit her near the children, **passing judgement** on her with ease. Their relationship matters little to him, all he wants is to **maintain the outward show of marriage**. He coldly rejects her, and the idea of loving her.

Torvald's response to learning of Nora's misdeed shows **how superficial this world is that values reputation above love. It also shows how pretence and self-preservation are very much a part of this place and these characters' lives.**

Nora Leaves

Krogstad returns Nora's contract to the Helmers, removing them from any danger.

When Krogstad's letter arrives, addressed to Nora, Torvald opens it. He reads the news and declares that he is saved before burning the letter and contract. **In this world, difficult things are best destroyed and not dwelt on.**

Now that his reputation is safe, Torvald's attitude to Nora changes. He tells Nora that he would hardly be a man if her feminine weakness did not make him love her even more. Now that the danger is passed he takes up his old role. **He is the doting husband once more, patronising his childish wife.**

However, Nora's attitude to her life has been forever changed by Torvald's reaction to learning of her forgery. She speaks plainly to him, confronting the failings of their marriage, saying that in their eight years of married life they have never spoken seriously about a single thing. Nora and Torvald have had **a superficial, meaningless marriage, conforming to society's expected roles of husband and wife, rather than building a meaningful relationship** together. She has been Torvald's doll wife, just as she was her father's doll baby. **Nora realises how limited she has been by having these female roles dictated by her father and husband.**

She decides to leave, to discover herself, a decision that rocks Torvald, who calls her mad and forbids her to leave. **Nora's decision shatters the rules of this world, where wives do as their husbands tell them.**

Nora's departure, leaving her husband, children, and home behind her, is shocking in this world that defines women as housewives,

mothers and carers. This is an unthinkable development in this society, seen in Torvald's reaction, where he tells her to think about her place in her home.

Notes on Literary Genre

A Doll's House is a play, and should be considered as a **live action performance**, taking place before an audience. In this sense, the audience is the fourth wall of the Helmer home, we have been invited into their house to witness the events of this **domestic drama** play out. The entire action of the play takes place in the Helmers' apartment, we are guests in this very personal space. As such, we are spectators or onlookers to the action as a whole, and are **not tied to a single character's perspective**, but respond to the words and deeds of each character before us.

The **setting and props** on stage create a **domestic**, middle class sense of wealth and comfort.

Nora and Torvald's opening conversation concerns debt and borrowing, **foreshadowing** significant issues that will yield greater significance later on.

The playwright makes use of **visual prompts and cues** to add to the story. The disarray of the Christmas tree as the play progresses may **symbolise** Nora and Torvald's fraying marriage, the dishevelment of their home suggesting the cracks that are beginning to show in their crumbling lives.

Similarly, Krogstad's letter is a **visual reminder** for the audience of Nora's dangerous situation. Seeing the letter, and the letterbox, reminds us of its shattering contents, **adding tension and anticipation** to the story.

The playwright makes good use of **pacing** throughout the play, the story never lags, there is always something happening, some **new complication** to further the plot. For example, Mrs Linde, Dr Rank and Krogstad each arrive and move the action forward. This is a feature of the play, characters arriving and adding to the action, progressing the story.

The play follows the **three act structure**, dividing the story into three parts: **the setup, the confrontation, and the resolution.** As characters are established, we learn of Nora's forgery, committed to save her husband's life. As the story progresses, Nora attempts to prevent the truth from coming to light, which it inevitably does in the story's **climax.** This **question of discovery**, and Torvald's reaction to learning of Nora's wrongdoing, provides much of the **tension** the audience experience.

Nora's arc is a compelling feature of the play. The **development of Nora's character from silly, childish featherbrain to independent, decisive woman is worth considering.** In some ways, the story is really Nora's, charting her **transformation** from silly pet to free woman.

Nora appears at first to be superficial and shallow, but her **backstory adds complexity to our understanding of her character.** She has hidden strength and grit, going to great lengths to save her husband's life and secretly earn an income to repay her debt to Krogstad.

She is loving and hopeful, placing complete faith in her husband's love for her, only to have this belief coldly destroyed by Torvald's selfish reaction to learning of her selfless crime.

It is Torvald's response to learning of her crime of forgery that is the catalyst for the change in Nora. **In a moment of high drama, Nora experiences an epiphany and realises the falseness of her married**

life. This realisation or **epiphany moment** completely changes Nora's understanding of her life and marriage, and is what **prompts her to abandon her home at the story's end.** This is an exciting and significant character development that adds to the narrative.

Torvald's weakness adds to the **emotional impact** of this scene, the audience sympathises with Nora whose husband is so lacking, after she has done so much for him.

Interesting **characterisation** extends to Krogstad, who is far from a stereotypical villain. He is a man in a tight spot, driven to desperate lengths, **not a typical villain.** The humanity and relatability of his character adds to its complexity, making him feel real and authentic.

Conflict makes the play tense and exciting, and very involving for the audience. **Secrets, and the threat of the truth being discovered promises conflict** in the story. **Tension** builds as Krogstad blackmails Nora and she attempts to conceal her crime from Torvald.

When the truth is discovered, Torvald's reaction reveals a startling truth to Nora, that Torvald is not the man she thought he was. Nora cannot remain with Torvald when she sees him for what he is, a **dramatic and conflict rich** moment in the story.

The play is dramatic, serious and impactful, with its outcome carrying weight and affecting the audience, who must decide whether they condone or condemn Nora's leaving. This makes the ending very involving and meaningful as the audience must make sense of Nora's actions and decide whether or not she did the right thing.

Literary Genre
Key Moments

Opening Scene

The play's opening scene establishes the **setting**, the Helmers' middle class home, and **introduces Nora and Torvald** to the audience. The **nature of their relationship is clear**; Torvald refers to Nora as being a silly, but expensive pet, and she fulfills her role, behaving very childishly. He comments on what a sweet little featherbrain she is, adding that it costs a lot to keep such a creature. Nora is his exotic, expensive pet.

Their **characters** are clear to the audience, Torvald plays the part of condescending, authoritative adult, speaking down to his disobedient child, asking if she was naughty in town, buying sweets. For Nora's part, she plays the role of a child and denies buying sweets, even though the audience have already seen her eating them. Their **roles within their marriage** are clearly seen.

The **themes of money and reputation** are also introduced, with an emphasis on how fortunate they are now that Torvald is being promoted. These significant themes will be developed further over the course of the play.

Mrs Linde Arrives and Speaks with Nora

The **arrival of Mrs Linde (Kristine), Nora's old friend, adds to the story's development, Nora's character and audience anticipation** as Nora reveals how she borrowed money to save her husband's life.

Nora tells Mrs Linde that she saved Torvald's life by getting money for the trip to Italy, but she does not reveal the details of how she did it, hinting that an admirer may have been the source of money at the time. This piques the audience's interest, making us want to know more about Nora's actions.

This scene introduces **threat** and the promise of Nora's actions being discovered, while also suggesting that Nora is a stronger, more determined **character** than she seemed at first.

Moments after Nora tells Mrs Linde these details from her past, Krogstad calls to speak to Nora. Nora's reaction to his presence alerts the audience to the fact that something is amiss, there is some **tension** between them concerning a **secret matter**. In this way, this scene adds excitement, while developing the plot and Nora's character. **The set-up is complete for escalating action as the narrative progresses.**

Krogstad Threatens Nora

Krogstad visits Nora towards the end of Act One to coerce her into keeping his job at the bank for him, asking her to use her influence over her husband for him. When she resists, **he threatens to expose her forgery. This is a tense moment**, but even as Krogstad threatens to expose Nora, he shows compassion and understanding too, saying that her transgression was nothing more than his own mistake.

Krogstad's threat to expose Nora brings threat, **conflict and suspense** to the play. The balance of power is in his favour, he will reveal everything to Torvald if Nora does not do as he wishes. This **manipulation and blackmail makes the story very engrossing and exciting**.

Even as Krogstad pressures Nora to keep his position at the bank, he is polite and courteous. **He is in a bind, driven by his desperation to regain respectability, rather than a malicious motivation**. The fact that Krogstad is not portrayed as being threatening or menacing grounds his character in reality and makes him feel real. His **characterisation** is a strength of the story, adding complexity and depth to the characters and their situation.

Krogstad's Letter

Krogstad's conversation with Nora in the second act is much more tense and highly charged than when they spoke in Act One. Matters are escalating as Nora grows closer to being exposed. Krogstad's letter to Torvald telling him the truth about **Nora's loan is a device the playwright uses to ratchet up the tension.** This letter will tell Torvald everything, a fate Nora is keen to avoid.

The mood darkens as Krogstad tells Nora that he owns her reputation. He tells her that running away, or even suicide, will not provide her with a way out. He mentions her body under the ice, adding a sense of **foreboding** to the scene. The **action is closing in on Nora**, moving the plotline forward to a point she resists. She exclaims that Krogstad has finished things for her and Torvald, an ominous statement. This is **gripping for the audience as we see Nora trapped by the truth. We must anxiously wait to see if Krogstad's threats will bear fruit, or if Nora will somehow find a way out.**

Torvald Discovers Nora's Crime

The moment of discovery is a very tense and exciting highpoint in

the play. This moment has been built up to, with Nora trying to delay it for as long as possible, adding to the **tension and audience anticipation.**

Another feature that has increased our **anticipation** of this moment is **Nora's anxiety.** On the one hand, she hopes a miracle will occur, on the other, she fears what will happen when the truth comes out. Her **fear adds to the tension**, as the audience shares her concern and wonders what will happen next. **Nora's thoughts are darker and more desperate as we approach the point where the truth is revealed,** Nora considers never seeing her children again and imagines herself in the deep, black water in the moments before Torvald discovers her crime. **This is the play's climax, a moment of excruciating tension.**

Torvald's harsh, self-centred reaction reveals his true self, as he calls Nora a criminal. He cares only about himself and his reputation, and is quick to say he no longer loves Nora, that he cannot trust her and will not allow her near their children. Torvald's behaviour here provokes anger and outrage in the **audience**, who feel for Nora who is treated with such scorn and contempt.

The Ending

Torvald's reaction spurs an **epiphany** in Nora, **she sees with absolute clarity what a sham her marriage is.** In a **dramatic moment** of insight, Nora realises that Torvald has never understood her and that she has been wronged by him and her father. This realisation is what causes Nora to dramatically walk out on Torvald, shattering society's conventions. As Nora chooses to find her own path in life, and no longer fulfil her empty roles of wife and mother, **the story reaches its resolution. The Helmer marriage cannot be repaired, the truth has destroyed it.**

The ending is **shocking and involving as the audience are forced to consider whether or not Nora did the right thing by walking out like this**. She leaves a changed woman from the one we met in Act One, **her transformation is complete**, another very involving and appealing feature of the narrative. Gone is Nora, the silly featherbrain, **her character has grown and developed over the course of the play**.

Notes on General Vision and Viewpoint

Ibsen offers a mixed outlook in 'A Doll's House', showing both the positives and negatives of life. There are **elements of positivity**, for example in Mrs Linde and Krogstad's renewed relationship and in Nora's brave decisiveness at the play's end. The playwright also **explores the darker side of life, presenting us with disappointment, deception, blackmail and hollow relationships**. He also raises interesting questions about truth in our lives, and whether it is a destructive or constructive force.

The way characters treat one another has a big bearing on the general vision and viewpoint of the play. When characters are false and self-centred their lives are shown to be hollow and empty. This is particularly true of Torvald and Nora's marriage which cannot withstand the strain of the truth of Nora's forgery. When faced with the prospect of the ruination of his reputation, Torvald reveals his selfish, self-centred, condescending nature. He is a **disappointment**, failing to be the man Nora hoped him to be.

To a lesser extent, sincerity and truthfulness in relationships are shown to yield happiness in life. Krogstad and Kristine's reunion demonstrates the redemptive and transformative power of love, giving these characters fresh **optimism** about life. Both Krogstad and Kristine had unhappy marriages, but when they commit to a relationship together, having discussed their past, their lives improve.

In the play, **Ibsen showcases the darker side of human nature. Krogstad's threats to Nora show how manipulative and single-minded people can be in getting what they want.** Krogstad blackmails Nora in an attempt to regain respectability, the contradiction of what he does is lost on him, but not on the audience. He threatens Nora in order to regain his upright social standing, thinking only of himself, not caring how his actions impact on Nora's life.

Life is shown to be devoid of purpose without someone to love in 'A Doll's House'. When Mrs Linde arrives she describes **how adrift and untethered she feels without someone to live for.** Later, when Mrs Linde meets Krogstad, this idea of needing someone to give purpose to your life is raised once more. Krogstad reveals Kristine previously broke his heart, rejecting him in favour of the rich man who became her husband. Their backstory shows why choices are made in life, in this instance Kristine chose the man who had the most to offer financially, a calculated take on marriage. **However, the possibility of a relationship with Krogstad is hopeful and shows the redemptive power of love.**

Mrs Linde admits her past mistakes. She is open and sincere, as Krogstad is with her. Through baring the truth and facing their issues, they agree to forge a life together. **The playwright suggests that when we are honest, love can succeed. There is optimism and positivity in this story strand as Mrs Linde and Krogstad's rekindled relationship transforms their lives and gives both characters the potential for great future happiness.** Such is the effect on Krogstad that he ceases to pursue the Helmers and returns Nora's contract. **Love changes him, a positive comment on human nature.**

At the play's end, Nora chooses to walk out on her life and discover who she truly is. **For Nora, living without a husband or family to care for is not a bleak option.** Although **life will be difficult alone**, this is the only way that Nora can discover who she is. **Choosing this path is necessary and leaving her husband, who has limited her in so many ways, may be seen as a triumph of sorts.**

Other aspects of the play add to the feeling that **life is difficult.** Mrs Linde tells Dr Rank that one has to live when he questions her about why someone overworked would want a job. Her answer shows the grim reality of her life and her **struggle for survival.**

Dr Rank's talk of **sick** and **morally ill patients** tends towards the **darker side of life.** He freely calls Krogstad depraved, happily passing this vicious judgement.

Dr Rank's illness and impending death also darkens the mood of the play. As he shuts himself away, Torvald is quick to forget about him and move on, looking forward to a time when it is just him and Nora. **His reaction here shows how false this friendship has been**, Rank was merely a pleasant distraction for Torvald, the connection lacked real sincerity, which **strikes a cold note for the audience.**

Similarly, when Rank reveals his love of Nora, she does not want to hear anything about it. She calls his profession of love clumsy, wishing she had never heard it. **Nora's offhand rejection of Rank adds to the background feeling of discontent and unhappiness in these characters' lives. There is a sense that life is full of trials and tribulations, from Torvald's breakdown to Rank's illness and Mrs Linde's hard life. Life is shown to be hard and trying.** However, these difficulties need not be overpowering when relationships are positive and rewarding, as illustrated by Krogstad and Mrs Linde and their open and sincere rekindled relationship. **It is when relationships fail, and characters are limited and denied their self-development and growth that life is seen to be hollow, a shadow of what it could be.** For Nora, both her father and husband have limited her, neither one recognising her self worth or helping her to reach her full potential

Ultimately, the outlook of the play's closing scene depends on whether the viewer feels Nora was right to leave her family and home behind and go into the world alone. Some may view her actions as brave and decisive and may see her as escaping the shackles of marriage to find her true self. Others may view her abandonment of her home and children as harsh and cold. Perhaps Ibsen is suggesting that **life choices are never easy and are not without their consequences. He may suggest that freedom, independence and happiness are possible, but are not necessarily easy to achieve.**

General Vision and Viewpoint
Key Moments

Nora's Conversation with Mrs Linde

Nora's conversation with her old friend shows **how hard life has been for Kristine.** When Mrs Linde (Kristine) calls to the house, Nora does not recognise her at first. Mrs Linde is greatly changed, having had a difficult time, including the loss of her husband, since Nora last saw her. **Kristine's appearance strikes a note of loss.** She has struggled since her husband's death, showing that **life can be hard and trying.** Nora describes Kristine

as **completely alone**, and says **how awful that must be**, stressing the
struggles and hardships she has endured.

Nora is insensitive to Kristine's loss and struggles. After inconsiderately
telling Kristine how rich she will be now that Torvald is the new bank
manager, she tells Kristine how hard things were when she was first
married.

She speaks of having to work, of Torvald's breakdown and need to travel
abroad to recover. She tells us that she was pregnant and her father was
dying. **This account is much more trying than the glowingly positive
life she has spoken of until now. This shows life's difficulties and
problems are everywhere.** In this case, they were overcome and things
improved. However, we will later learn that Nora managed to save Torvald's
life through forging a contract for a loan from Krogstad, something she
has kept a secret all this time. **The playwright will ask us to consider
whether one can ever escape a lie, if one's life is built on it.**

Mrs Linde married her now deceased husband to provide financially for
her sick mother and younger brothers. It was a union borne not of love, but
duty towards her family. This is a disheartening fact, showing that **money
trumps love in this world. Mrs Linde had to be practical rather than
emotional in order to survive, which darkens the outlook here.**

Mrs Linde now feels **purposeless and adrift**. Her mother has died, her
brothers are grown, there is nobody depending on her any longer. **Feeling
empty, she searches for work to give meaning to her life.** This is a
**bleak outlook, Mrs Linde has spent her life caring for others, and
now is left with nothing but a void in her life. Without someone to
look after, her life feels hollow and meaningless.**

Kristine describes her situation as one that makes you hard. She realises she has become harder because of the tough times she has endured.

Nora tells Kristine that it is she who saved Torvald's life. She reveals how she saved Torvald as she wants Kristine to take her seriously. She says **Torvald is never to know, as it would break them apart if he felt he owed her anything.** This shows **the fragility of imperfect love,** Nora feels **their marriage could not bear the truth of what she has done to save his life.**

Nora says that **she may reveal her secret one day, when she is older and Torvald is less taken with her.** This is a very **calculating move** that **detracts from the idea of saving a life for love.** The audience must wonder at the depth of Torvald's love that his wife feels the need to have something to hold influence over him in declining years. This is a rather **sad thought** for a couple that have shared their lives together.

Rank's Illness

Following Torvald's dismissal of Nora's pleas not to fire Krogstad, we learn that Rank is suffering from a terminal illness. **His sickness turns our thoughts to mortality and death, a dark, morbid turn.** As pressure increases on Nora, the audience is shown how difficult and trying life can be. **The outlook becomes more grim as Nora's situation worsens.**

Rank plans to shut himself away once his decline begins. He describes his death as being for someone else's guilt, an unfair price to pay for his father's sins. His spine has to pay for his father's indulgences. Nora, trying to change the subject, speaks of food. **She shows an inability here to talk about something that really matters, choosing to focus on trivialities. This suggests her friendship with Rank is false and hollow**, she cannot talk to him about something so serious, that matters so much.

Dr. Rank reveals his love for Nora, which displeases her. She says it was uncalled for, unhappy that he has told her how he feels. She calls him clumsy, finding the moment and unwanted declaration of love awkward. **His feelings seem to matter little, a difficult fact of life here.**

Later, Torvald will easily accept the news of Rank's pending death, calling into question the strength of his friendship with the doctor. **Torvald processes Rank's approaching death with ease, showing the falseness of his connection with the man. His coldness and indifference show how lacking and empty human bonds can be, a saddening comment on life.**

Krogstad Threatens Nora a Second Time

Krogstad, having lost his job at the bank, visits Nora a second time. He tells her that Torvald must reinstate him in a better position in the bank. He is not prepared to lose his job and attempts to **manipulate and blackmail** Nora to get what he wants.

Putting Nora under presure to do what he wants, he **refers to running away and suicide to scare and coerce her.** He talks about her body floating under the ice, gruesomely describing her bloated corpse.

Krogstad has trapped Nora, something he highlights by speaking of suicide. **He is cold and calculating here.** Nora has no option but to do as he says, he tells her that he owns her reputation. **In this tense moment Nora's future looks grim.**

Krogstad insists that Torvald will get his letter revealing everything. Interestingly, Krogstad adds that this is all Torvald's doing, that Krogstad was forced into it. **He does not see himself as a villain, but as a hard-pressed father, struggling to become respectable for his sons' sakes. Krogstad shows us the dark measures we are capable of when in a bind.** He is willing to destroy Nora to get what he wants. The **darker side of humanity** and the **drive for self-preservation** are clearly seen in Krogstad's actions. However, his motivation is one of love for his family. His humanity is clear, even as he takes on this dark role of manipulator.

Mrs Linde Talks to Krogstad

Kristine's conversation with Krogstad reveals some of the details of their past, and how she broke his heart when she left him to marry a richer man. She explains that financial stability was her motivation, showing that **the reason for marriage is not always love.**

Nils (Krogstad) describes his anguish when she left him, saying he was shipwrecked when she left.

Kristine says they are two drowning people and asks Krogstad to give her something to work for. She knows all about his past, and his dealings with the Helmers, but says she trusts the man he really is. She wants to be a mother to his children, and says her and Nils need each other. Kristine is totally open and honest here, as is Krogstad. There are no secrets between them. **Kristine needs Krogstad to give purpose to her life.**

There is hope and redemption in this reunion. Kristine and Nils now have a **second chance** at a life together, at a chance for happiness. They have both made mistakes in the past, and their openness and acceptance of one another is a very positive feature of their relationship. Krogstad no longer wants to exert power over Torvald, nor does he want to punish Kristine for leaving him before. **The redemptive power of love, and the hope it inspires is clear, showing the positive side of life.**

Krogstad says he will ask for his letter back, Nora's salvation is now possible. However, Mrs Linde says that Torvald must read the letter. She says there must be no more secrets and lies, that Nora and Torvald need to understand one another.

Mrs Linde's decision not to save her friend is an interesting one. It could be interpreted as meddling, unkind or unfair, that rather than save her friend, Mrs Linde insists on Torvald's discovery of Nora's crime. However, Mrs Linde is actually acting in Nora's best interests here. **She realises how false Nora's marriage is, and knows that the truth is necessary for Nora and Torvald to confront the reality of their lives.** Facing one's problems calls for bravery, and so Mrs Linde is doing her friend a service in feeling that the truth must come out, knowing that Nora will cope with the consequences. **Mrs Linde's actions demonstrate Ibsen's outlook that the truth must come to light, Nora must see the reality of the life she lives in order to be free to discover her own identity.**

Torvald Turns on Nora

Torvald's discovery of Nora's crime of forgery was to be Nora's 'miracle', the moment when Torvald proved himself to be the man she believed he was. She hoped that Torvald would take the burden of her forgery on himself, wanting to protect her, such was the depth of the love he always claimed to have for her. Torvald's discovery of the contents of the letter is necessary for

Nora to face the reality of her life, for her husband's reaction is far from that of an adoring, devoted husband.

As Torvald reads his mail we see Nora put her shawl over her head, saying she will never see her children again and speaking of deep, black water. When he stops her as she leaves the house Nora says, "You won't save me, Torvald." However, **saving Nora is not what Torvald plans to do.**

Instead, **his first thoughts are of himself.** He tells Nora to stop playing games and calls her a criminal, saying he should have expected it of her. Here, he is self-centred and cruel. **Ibsen shows us how selfish people can be when faced with danger and adversity. The facade of their loving marriage has crumbled to nothing. Torvald cares only for himself, his disregard for Nora shows how empty of meaning their life together has been.**

Torvald accuses Nora of killing his happiness and destroying his future, saying he is now at Krogstad's mercy. **He pities himself for his bleak future.**

Nora responds by saying that when she is out of the way he will be free. Torvald dismisses her words, saying that her being out of the way would not help him as Krogstad will tell his tale and people will assume Torvald knew of the matter. He shows no regard for Nora or how she is feeling, all his thoughts are of himself. **Through Torvald, the playwright shows us how empty and hollow relationships can be. It is difficult not to feel that Nora has wasted her life with this man who is so self-absorbed and cares so little for her.**

This moment of conflict has shed light on Torvald's true character, and he is found lacking. He says the matter must be hushed up, whatever it costs, telling Nora that they will maintain the appearance of their marriage, but that he cannot trust her near their children again. **Torvald's condescension is infuriating. It is a dark comment on life that he is so self-centred and understands his wife, and what she has done for him, so little.**

Nora Leaves

Torvald receives a letter from Krogstad and declares himself saved. Krogstad's life has changed now that he has found love with Mrs Linde and he longer pursues the Helmers. Although a minor point in comparison to what is unfolding in the Helmer household, Krogstad's actions here demonstrate the **redemptive power of love.** Krogstad and Mrs Linde have been open and honest with one another, and **their love story gives reason to be optimistic about life.**

Krogstad's actions cause a complete reversal in Torvald. Now that he is saved, his thoughts are of Nora and how dreadful the past three days have been for her. He forgives her and realises that what she did was done out of love for him. What he does not realise however, is that a great change has come over Nora. **Having seen her husband for who he really is, she cannot revert to how things were before** he learned of her forgery. **She has experienced an epiphany, and cannot now unsee the reality of her marriage and life.**

Nora speaks of the falseness of their relationship, how they have never spoken seriously about a single thing in their eight years together. **Nora tells Torvald that he never loved her,** that it was the idea of loving her that pleased him, as it did her father. She says she has been like a beggar, existing to perform for him. **Her words show how empty and shallow** her life with Torvald has been. Society's patriarchal structure has denied Nora the chance to discover who she is, to live her life to her full potential. Her life has been limited by those who should have loved and supported her most, a wretched truth.

Now that Nora has experienced an epiphany and seen Torvald for what he is, she chooses to leave him and go into the world alone. Whether or not this moment is one of hope or sorrow depends to a degree on the audience's outlook. On one hand, Nora's brave decision to leave is a very positive and optimistic moment. Now she will have the chance to become independent, free of her false marriage and overbearing husband.

On the other hand, the fact that she leaves her children behind has earned her much criticism. Leaving them here with this man she calls a 'stranger' suggests coldness or lack of feeling towards them.

However, before leaving she tells Torvald that he was right when he said she could never teach the children. She feels that she must bring herself up first. Perhaps Nora cannot take on responsibility for her children too as she leaves to go into the world alone. She is not rejecting them as such, rather she knows that she must leave, alone, and make her way in the world.

Ultimately, the way she speaks openly and honestly with Torvald and forsakes her empty life can be considered a success in itself. Nora is not afraid of her future, but embraces her new life, whatever it may be. Leaving her children behind prevents this moment from being entirely positive, but her resolve and bravery in leaving is very hopeful as she welcomes her future, free of the constraints of a marriage where she was stifled and limited. The outlook is positive as Nora leaves to make her way in the world.

Notes on Theme/Issue - Relationships

The play focuses on relationships, particularly **Nora and Torvald's flawed marriage**. The story charts the changing relationship of Nora and Torvald and shows the impact this relationship has on these characters and their lives.

As the story begins, Torvald speaks down to his wife and treats her as a favourite pet or child, a part that she seems happy to play, as he calls her songbird and little squirrel. However, this role of passive, submissive woman, told what to think and how to behave, is one that Nora rejects by the play's end. **Their marriage is forever changed by Torvald's reaction to Krogstad's letter, and Nora's response to Torvald's cold, self-centred outlook.**

In this text, **relationships are not what they appear to be**. Nora and Torvald's marriage is revealed to be **a marriage of stranger**s and their **friendship with Dr Rank also proves false**. What appear at first to be firm bonds are revealed to be insubstantial and worthless.

The **fake, false construct of relationships** is evident in the way that Nora does not really know Torvald, imagining him to be a better man than he is, capable of a 'miracle'. When she discovers the real nature of their relationship, realising the gulf between them despite their years of marriage, she feels compelled to leave. Torvald is not the man she imagined him to be.

It is not just romantic relationships that the play calls into question, but also the ties of friendship. Nora is unaware of Dr Rank's feelings for her, when he reveals his true emotions, he ruins their relationship for her. Without the pretence of him hiding his feelings, their **friendship collapses**.

Torvald's ease at dropping Rank when he learns of his illness is also noteworthy, making the audience question the sincerity of his friendship. He tells Nora that now it is just the two of them, untroubled by the loss of his friend.

There is **an element of fantasy to Nora and Torvald's marriage**. Torvald encourages Nora to dress up to dance the tarantella, delighting in the idea of playing at being someone else, of **imagining a different version of their relationship** where they are secret lovers. This idea of fantasy, or imagining who his wife is, can be applied in a broader sense. **Torvald sees Nora's title of wife as a character defining role, a life-controlling label, determining who she is.**

Despite the flaws in their marriage, it is worth noting that **Nora really loved Torvald** to go to the lengths she did to save his life. **She missed her father dying and committed forgery for Torvald's sake**. Not only this, she has coped with this problem alone, secretly paying back the debt to protect him.

Nora played the part of little songbird as Torvald took delight in it. Nora truly loves her husband, until the moment when his true, selfish self is revealed.

In this way we see that **relationships in the play suffer when they are too real or too demanding**. When Nora needs Torvald in a more than superficial way, he crumbles, just as Nora and Torvald fail Dr Rank when he turns to them in his darkest hour. **When relationships are false and superficial, they are shown to lack strength or the ability to endure.**

Nora's role as mother is also worth considering under the theme of relationships. She appears to enjoy spending time with her children, yet she walks out on them, leaving them with a man she calls a stranger. This makes us question the strength of her bond with her children. To leave them like this can be viewed as a cold, unfeeling action.

Not all relationships in the play are negative however. **The relationship between Krogstad and Mrs Linde is redemptive, changing him and offering him another chance at love and life.** Although this relationship is not as significant as that of Torvald and Nora, it does give some balance to this theme.

Theme/Issue - Relationships
Key Moments

Opening Scene

As the play begins, **Torvald speaks fondly of Nora, as if she is a favourite pet.** He calls her featherbrain, and speaks condescendingly to her, saying it costs a lot of pennies to keep a pet like her. She is a child in his eyes, lacking responsibility and understanding. He chides her for eating sweets, something she denies, fulfilling **her role of wayward child in need of discipline and instruction.** This is Nora's role in the relationship, she is like a pet or small child, something to be kept and fussed over, cute and entertaining, but lacking the depth and intellect of an adult. **Torvald's role is that of master or father, he is the one to make the decisions and assume responsibility, he is the dominant one in the relationship.**

Torvald describes the three weeks Nora spent making decorations last year as dull and boring. For him, **she is a distraction and a source of entertainment.**

Krogstad Threatens Nora

The relationship between Nora and Krogstad is interesting, as he has the power to ruin her by revealing her crime of forgery.

However, on a surface level, as the wife of his boss, Krogstad should be polite and deferential towards Nora. He is very courteous at the end of the first act when he comes to see her, despite insisting that she help him or he will ruin her, "if I lose everything a second time, you keep me company."

It is interesting how open and honest Nora is in her conversation with Krogstad, telling him truths she could never reveal to her husband, admitting to signing her father's name on their contract. In dealing **with Krogstad, Nora deals with an equal**, someone she has entered into a business arrangement with. Despite the power he holds over her because of her forgery, she speaks openly with him, concealing nothing. Her open approach with Krogstad highlights the constraints she feels in her marriage, what she reveals to Krogstad she hopes to keep hidden from Torvald, saying it would be awkward if Krogstad were to tell Torvald the truth. **In business she may be open and honest, but in her marriage she must hide the truth to protect her relationship, a significant contrast.**

Nora knows Torvald would not approve of what she has done, so she has kept it from him, not wanting any friction between them. Her secrecy and lack of honesty suggests a flawed marriage, where problems are buried deep.

Dr Rank Confesses His Love for Nora

Dr Rank reveals that he loves Nora, a very unwanted moment in

their relationship. Nora enjoys Dr Rank's company, until he reveals how he feels about her. **Once the playful pretence of their relationship gives way to reveal real emotion, Nora shies away.**

Nora is perturbed, and tells him his words were uncalled for. She changes from calling the doctor her truest, dearest friend, to calling him clumsy after he admits his love. This revelation is awkward in Nora's eyes, showing the **shallow nature of their friendship.** Nora is not prepared to discuss how Rank feels, their friendship is not as deep as we have thought.

As with his illness, Nora does not want to discuss anything serious or difficult. This gives insight into relationships in this text, **where serious matters are avoided, allowing relationships to be shallow and superficial.**

Nora's attitude is echoed in Torvald's response to learning of Rank's illness and imminent death. Discovering that Rank intends to shut himself away from the world to die, he responds that it may be for the best, for them as well as for him. **Torvald's reaction is cold and self-interested, he does not spare Rank a second thought.**

It is also worth noting the dramatic, romantic way Torvald views his relationship with Nora, as if they are romantically cut off from the world, rather than being parents running a household. **There is an element of fantasy in how he views his marriage.**

Krogstad Comes to Speak to Mrs Linde

Krogstad and Mrs Linde's relationship contrasts with that of Nora and Torvald. Both Kristine and Krogstad have had unhappy marriages, they do not view married life as a romantic dream. As they talk, we realise they had a relationship in the past, with Kristine choosing a rich man over Nils to secure financial stability for her family. This was a pragmatic choice, not a choice of the heart.

Despite Kristine having hurt Nils in the past, there is the possibility of moving forwards and loving each other again. She asks him to give her someone and something to work for.

Mrs Linde feels adrift and purposeless without someone to love and care for. **A meaningful relationship would give shape and focus to her life**, showing how important relationships are to these characters.

Mrs Linde and Krogstad have suffered heartbreak and unhappiness, but their openness and sincerity makes another chance at love possible. They speak frankly to one another, creating the hope of a future together.

This relationship shows that **meaningful relationships are possible, when people are open, honest and forgiving. They add a positive note to the theme of relationships in the text, contrasting with the fake, superficial relationships of the Helmer household.**

Torvald's Reaction to Nora's Crime

Before Torvald learns of Nora's forgery and loan, she tells Mrs Linde that a "miracle" is about to take place, **believing that Torvald will not react negatively towards her**. He says himself that he has often wished Nora were in some deadly danger so that he could save her. He sounds deeply committed, wishing for an opportunity to express his devotion to Nora.

However, **when Torvald learns the truth of what Nora has done, he turns on her**, speaking of lies and deceit and calling her a criminal. He says he should have expected it, a very damning statement, and accuses his wife of killing his happiness and destroying his future. **Torvald's real attitude to his wife is revealed in these telling moments, when he sees her as a burden and a problem. In this moment of crisis all thoughts are of himself.**

He tells Nora that the pretence of their marriage will be maintained in public, that she will continue to live in their home, but that he shall not permit her near the children. **Torvald's rejection of Nora is swift and complete**, he maps out the course their sham marriage will take from this point on. **He shows how empty and loveless their marriage really is in this moment of pressure.**

When a letter arrives from Krogstad sending back Nora's forged contract, Torvald exclaims that he is saved. His thoughts are of himself first, a truth that Nora can no longer ignore. **This episode has a huge impact on Nora, revealing to her the true nature of the man she married, and the true reality of her false marriage. It is Nora's insight that spells the end for their relationship, for she can no longer devote her life to this man.**

Nora Leaves

Nora's decision to walk out on her life, leaving behind her home and family, tells us a lot about her relationship with her husband. She realises that she has been passed from father to husband, and has never fully realised her own potential.

Nora realises how empty and lacking the significant relationships in her life have been, saying that Torvald and her father never really loved her, but rather were pleased by the idea of loving her. Torvald's cold reaction has made her aware of how flawed her marriage is, and she does not want to stay with a man who cannot love her.

Nora feels let down and cheated by the men who should have cared most. She realises she has existed to perform for Torvald, and that both Torvald and her father have blocked her life. **Nora sees how her life has been limited by the roles she was expected to play and conform to.**

Torvald is shocked and panicked by Nora's words and implores her to stay, even forbidding her to leave. Nora replies that there shall be no more forbidding, that she will take her things and needs nothing of his, now or later. **Her rejection of Torvald, and her role as his wife, is complete and absolute**. His authority counts for nothing. She wants nothing more to do with this man who has let her down so badly, and failed to be the loving husband she imagined him to be.

Torvald cannot understand what is happening, telling Nora that she is not making any sense. Nora explains that she saw his true self when the miracle did not happen and he failed to be the man she thought he was. He fails to understand how he has failed Nora, saying that no man sacrifices his honour for the one he loves. **He cannot conceive of the self-sacrifice and devotion that Nora has given, failing to be the husband Nora longed for**. She recognises the faults and failings of their marriage and chooses to leave.

As the play closes, Nora says she does not know Torvald, refusing to spend the night in a strange man's house, negating all their years of marriage. **She rejects her empty marriage and selfish husband.**

Nora's relationship with her children is worth examining in this moment. She leaves them behind with her husband, this stranger, and goes alone into the world, saying that she does not want to see them. She severs every bond with her home before leaving, telling Torvald that they are both free. **While leaving her children like this may trouble the audience, it shows how completely Nora needs to free herself from Torvald and live her own life.** She says that the woman she is now can do nothing for them. Her role of mother is less important than her desire to leave and discover herself.

Notes on Hero, Heroine, Villain (Ordinary Level)

At the start of the play Nora appears as a silly, foolish girl, with little strength or substance to her character. She enjoys Torvald's pet names for her and plays the part of pet or child to his role of master or parent. She is needy and dependant, viewing him as the superior, dominant one in their marriage, someone she must please and pander to, while he makes the important decisions.

However, **over the course of the play, Nora grows and develops, transforming into a strong, determined woman by the play's final moments.** It turns out that **she is tougher and more self-reliant than we may think.** Like Torvald, we underestimate her. When we learn that Nora has saved Torvald's life and that she has worked secretly for months to pay an illegal debt, she grows in our estimation. **Nora has hidden depths and is more determined, resilient and tough than we may have realised at first, weathering Torvald's illness and her father's death with only herself to rely on.**

When Torvald learns of Nora's crime and turns on her, Nora has an **epiphany**. Suddenly, **she sees Torvald and her flawed marriage clearly,** telling her husband that he does not understand her and that she has never understood him until now. She is calm and reasonable as she explains to Torvald how he has failed her and why she is leaving. **She is completely transformed from the silly woman we met in the first act.**

However, although Nora grows in our estimation over the course of the story, **she remains a problematic character because of the way she walks out on her life at the end of the play.** Her willingness to leave not just her home and husband, but also her young children, can cause audiences to react negatively to her and her decision to leave on a journey of self-discovery.

As the play ends, Nora does not fully know who she is, but she has shown bravery and courage in her decision to cast off her old life and discover who she can become.

Hero/Heroine/Villain (Ordinary Level) Key Moments

Opening Scene

Nora appears silly and childish as the play begins, happily responding to Torvald's pet names of songbird and squirrel.

She is excited about Christmas, planning the gifts she will buy for the children. She tells her husband that the gift she would really like for Christmas is some pennies of her own, showing that she is **dependant** on her husband and **does not have financial independence or income** of her own. Torvald calls her a sweet featherbrain, saying it is expensive to keep a pet like her, showing that she is not Torvald's equal.

Another aspect of the opening scene that makes Nora seem childish is the way **she sneakily eats forbidden sweets, and then lies about it. This childish act makes her seem very silly, irresponsible and child-like.**

Meeting Mrs Linde

Although she does not recognise her old friend at first, **Nora is happy to see Kristine and welcomes her warmly.** She mentions reading of the death of Mrs Linde's husband, saying she meant to write to her but never got around to it. Her words here show how she failed her friend, how she knew she should make contact and never did. This shows that **Nora is busy, but also self-centred.**

Nora is also selfish and inconsiderate when she hears of Kristine's hardships and difficulties, turning the conversation to how wonderful her own life will be once Torvald starts his new job in the New Year. Nora speaks of having lots of money, having just heard of Mrs Linde's problems and lack of financial support.

Nora reveals her secret to her old friend, showing her trusting nature and innocence, as she boasts of saving her husband's life. This secret shows how much she loves Torvald, but also suggests strength of character and determination that we have not seen up to this point.

Playing Hide & Seek With the Children

Nora enjoys chatting and playing hide and seek with her children,

laughing and running around the room with them. **She is a fun parent**, and her children delight in her company. However, **she calls them 'dolly-babies', suggesting she is playing the role of mother**, and they are her doll children.

The fact that Anne-Marie provides most of the children's care may also compromise how we view Nora as a mother. She enjoys playing with them, but her children are a responsibility that Nora is used to handing over to someone else.

Standing up to Krogstad

When Krogstad comes to see Nora at the end of the first act, she is apprehensive, saying that it is not time for him to collect his monthly debt. Despite feeling anxious about his arrival, **Nora speaks openly and honestly with Krogstad.** When he asks whether Mrs Linde has been given a job at the bank, she gives him the information he needs, even though she knows he should not ask questions like these as he is an employee of Torvald's. Nora shows an awareness of society's rules about what one can and cannot say and do, but she is not bound by them, choosing to give Krogstad his answer.

It is interesting that Nora admits her forgery to Krogstad here, something she has yet to tell Torvald about. **This shows that in the world of business, she sees herself as Krogstad's equal, someone she can be open with, whereas in her marriage, she has to conceal certain truths about herself.** She says that Torvald finding out would be awkward, showing an **awareness of poor communication in her relationship with her husband.**

Nora's reason for forging her father's signature is significant. She was saving her dying father from care and worry by keeping her situation from him while secretly borrowing to save Torvald's health. **Nora plays the role of carer to the men in her life.**

In her exchange with Krogstad, there is much to admire in Nora's character. She is **brave, outspoken and honest**, she is not cowed by the threat and power he holds over her. In this scene another layer of Nora's character is revealed, **she is more than a silly wife doting on her husband.**

Belief in Torvald Dashed - A Moment of Epiphany

A great change comes over Nora when she discovers Torvald's true, self-centred nature. When he learns of her crime and thinks only of himself her view of him changes forever. When she tells him that he meant all the world to her, he dismisses her love, focusing on his loss of reputation. His reaction brings about a moment of epiphany for Nora. She has a moment of startling insight where **she realises who Torvald really is and what her life with him has been.**

Nora realises how empty their relationship has been, saying that he has never understood her. Nora is decisive and brave in the way she acts on her realisation and chooses to leave Torvald and make a life for herself, something unheard of in this society. **Her realisation shows wisdom and understanding, while her choice shows bravery and determination.**

Nora Leaves

Nora is a very different person as the play ends, to who she was in the beginning. **Gone is the silly featherbrain, replaced by an independent, decisive woman**, who is choosing to discover a new life for herself.

She is calm and unemotional as she tells Torvald that she must go, unable to spend the night in a strange man's house. Gone are the play and pretence, the laughter and pet names. Nora is confident and final as she says goodbye to Torvald, telling him that she does not want to see the children. With her words, **she completely rejects her roles of wife and mother**, stating that now they are both free. **She does not see herself as abandoning her old life, but rather as starting afresh**, free to make her own choices and decisions.

The way that Nora leaves her children behind with Torvald is problematic. It is difficult to see her as entirely heroic when she leaves them with this man that she calls a stranger. However, she states that she cannot bring them up, having to focus on discovering who she is first. She is **aware of her need to be independent and discover truths about herself**, and this is a courageous idea.

Lightning Source UK Ltd.
Milton Keynes UK
UKHW040725140222
398653UK00001B/3